PROVENÇAL LIVING

First published in the United Kingdom in 2007 by Scriptum Editions
an imprint of Co & Bear Productions (UK) Ltd

ISBN-10 1 902 686 61 6
ISBN-13 978 1 902 686 61 5

Publisher Beatrice Vincenzini & Francesco Venturi
Executive Director David Shannon
Design Brian Rust

First edition
1 3 5 7 9 10 8 6 4 2

Printed in Italy

PROVENÇAL LIVING

PHOTOGRAPHY BY ANDREAS VON EINSIEDEL

SCRIPTUM EDITIONS

Much has been written about Provence – the most visited and acclaimed region of France – so it is surprising to find that people still disagree about where the ancient province begins and ends. Its boundaries, which moved constantly throughout centuries of invasion, were fixed in 1947, so geographically speaking it lies between Italy in the east, and beyond the great waterway of the Rhône to the west. Yet, to many Parisians their Provence (the real Provence) is a 'golden triangle' from Avignon and Arles to Aix-en-Provence and nominally the westerly side of the Lubéron. There is passion and possession in every argument, and for all Provençaux – and, indeed, recent arrivals – the boundaries will continue to expand and contract.

Although outwardly much changed by industry, tourism and highways, the essential unwavering attraction remains undiluted. Ringed by broken and often desolate mountain ranges, these ancient natural fortifications define the quality of light and vegetation and, along with the Durance and Rhône rivers, provided the protection, warmth and water that were (and largely still are to this day) the region's lifeblood, first agricultural and now touristic. Many smaller limestone ridges run east and west within the outer mountain ranges, and – though relatively easy to quarry – the pale, malleable stone has endured, defining Provençal architecture from the humble *cabanon* (country cottage) to the grand chateau. The old elements of architecture remain and live on, be they gently sloping roofs covered in Roman tiles, traditional wooden shutters or limewash colours echoing the natural pigments of the earth.

AN OLD farmhouse
with thick rubble-stone
walls and a clay-tiled
roof, nestles in gently
rolling provençal
landscape. A hardy,
climbing rose thrives
on the north wall.

HIGH ABOVE ground level a small terrace with far-reaching views over a forest and the outer ring of village houses. At the end of an alleyway, a door opens on to a tiny, pebbled entrance courtyard. Behind the fruit picker's ladder is one of the original gateways into the old town and, just beyond the elegant fountain, a set of stone steps leads to the front door.

A TYPICAL PROVENÇAL roofline of terracotta-
tiled roofs and brick chimney stacks. The
weathered and moss-covered tiles forming a
patchwork of earthy colours.

CLIMBING ROSES will soon form a tunnel on the approach to the north end of the house. Careful landscaping has ensured there are outdoor living areas off all the main rooms, and old bed frames cut in half were originally used as day beds during the grape pickers' *vendange* (harvest).

A SIMPLE, STONE-EDGED swimming pool has been set into a newly created terrace slightly above the level of the house. From the freestanding gate, the river-pebble path leads to the kitchen terrace.

15

SHUTTERED WINDOWS are to be found all over Provence and potted plants are set out on every available surface, filtering bright light through climbing greenery or adding bold colour throughout the summer.

BEAUTIFULLY FORMED arches and narrow passages
leading off the ground-floor courtyard indicate how
the house might have linked to its neighbours in the
past. In deep shadow, with three floors rising above
it, this is a cool and private retreat during the hottest
days of summer.

A SILVERY green shuttered kitchen window typically opens straight on to the street in country villages. The choice of paint colour varies here from vivid lavender to ox-blood red and every known shade of blue and green.

A SINGLE, enormous tree acting as an umbrella shades the enclosed garden. Hugging the stone walls are massed plantings of hydrangea mixed with clipped, potted box and petunias. A tiny fountain trickles in one corner, and beyond the wall is an orchard and open farmland.

A FRENCH *HAMEAU* (hamlet) near Uzés, comprising a group of houses and barns, cottages, stables, and often a *pigeonnier*, all of which were interrelated and often co-dependent.

25

BOTH THE ENTRANCE front, shown on the previous page, and the expansive formal gardens behind feature large antique pots, stone and terracotta sphinxes and busts, statues, vases and topiary birds and animals.

THE FORMAL GARDEN seen from the staircase-landing window demonstrates the elegant geometry applied to the numerous "rooms" and enclosures through careful planting. Elegant iron gates open on to an enclosed gravel terrace immediately behind the house, which in turn leads through to the first of the formal garden "rooms".

A SPRING-FED pond at the rear of the garden is watched over by a Florentine wild boar fountain. A pair of dramatic, red Anglo-Chinese benches provides a shock of colour and surprise in this largely green and white garden. Most Provençal houses have a bell to announce one's arrival at the side door.

THIS BEAUTIFULLY MADE, grand stone arch, that would have once been the main entrance to the farm complex, leads into the central courtyard.

A SWEEPING TERRACE contains an impressively large pool and covered entertaining space with kitchen, changing rooms and showers. The spectacular view encompasses *Mont Ventoux* in the distance and deep terraces are swathed with roses.

ROSES SCENT THE AIR at every turn. Gateposts and terraces, arbors and walkways are smothered in white, cream, pink and golden roses of dazzling variety. The approach to the house is lined with clipped hedges, cypress and a field of old olive trees. Hundreds of cypress, once used only as tightly planted wind-breaks, are now a key vertical statement in modern Provençal gardens.

OUTSIDE STEPS were a common feature
of old farm buildings. Mostly in
shadow, these ancient mossy stones
lead to the top of a barn constructed
of rough-hewn stone.

41

THE ONLY ENTRANCE to this courtyard
house and garden is through a large set
of curved and painted gates set into a
stone wall. Once a barren farmyard,
every centimeter of space has been
carefully terraced and planted with
sweet-smelling herbs and flowers.

ONE OF several, tiny original openings in the barn wall. Pergola covered seating areas abound and, in such a sheltered setting, meals are taken outdoors most of the year. The entrance to the guest quarters is slightly Italianate in its design.

TWO SEMICIRCLES of pencil-thin cypress
mark out lavender beds above the
swimming pool, rose arches form
gateways between each section of the
garden. The secret garden paved with a
calcade, a pebbled pathway whose
design was inspired by the *Topkapi*
palace in Istanbul.

MOUGINS MEDIEVAL PEDESTARIAN STREETS are narrow, with houses tightly grouped along and within the old walls. Originally built 900 years ago, there is clear evidence that – for defence – internal doors linked the dwellings.

49

PROTECTED ON THREE SIDES by the house and a cliff face on the fourth, this vivid blue courtyard emerges as a complete surprise, seen only from the windows at the back of the kitchen and sitting room. Furnished almost like a room, with a mosaic-topped table, iron chairs and day bed softened with bright cotton cushions and Chinese ceramic stools, the space is a true extension to the house.

AS MUCH A VIEWING PLATFORM as a summer dining room, the cane-covered, raised terrace has an uninterrupted view all the way to Marseille, across rolling terraces of lavender. Rendered concrete seating is covered with striped cushions and Moroccan lanterns are lit in the evenings.

LINKED TO THE HOUSE by a custom-made metal trellis smothered in
wisteria, the curtained outdoor kitchen is used throughout the summer.
Provençal houses usually have several shaded dining or reading areas,
positioned to be cool in summer but bright throughout the winter.
English teak chairs by Charles Verey have weathered to a deep silver
grey. The ceramic tree trunk table is Victorian. The bedrooms have
full-height windows overlooking a canopy of sculptural plane trees
and the *Alpilles* beyond.

LIMESTONE GATE PIERS support an elegant, but weather-beaten pair of painted gates. The entrance to the house was moved away from the front of the house, allowing a view along the terrace over the original well to a fountain placed at right angles to the house. A red rose growing outside is the only splash of colour in the largely silver, green and white scheme.

ON A TOPIARY TERRACE, quirky shapes
are silhouetted against the pale
facade and create convivial seating
areas. Modern teak furniture is
weathering to a silver-grey colour
in the sun, but at the kitchen end
a traditional metal frame is covered
in vines and creepers, providing
summer shade.

61

AN OCHRE-WASHED WALL links the house to a garden room, creating a private seating area before opening on to a wide border in the formal garden. A view from the main entrance doors over the raised topiary garden (opposite). The terrace fills the entire width of the house, providing several seating areas opening off the kitchen.

SEEN FROM A BEDROOM BALCONY, the formal
garden is reminiscent of a vivid Persian carpet.
Hundreds of clipped box drums edge beds of
clashing summer colours comprised of
petunias, dahlias, cosmos daisies and verbena,
and columns of cypress line the central path.

AN OLD RUN-DOWN COTTAGE that has been restored for guests but centuries-old, rare, carved-stone feeding troughs were found underneath. Vines surround the house on all sides, with forest beyond. The garden clings close to the cottage but plans to develop the gardens further are well under way.

A HEAVY STONE DOOR-FRAME links the dining room and grand salon to the entrance hall. The formal dining room is lined with French *chinoiserie* panels that had languished in storage for decades. Italian painted and caned chairs surround a Louis XVII-style table decorated with painted Masonic symbols, and through the old-fashioned fabric-lined door is the large farmhouse kitchen.

THESE VAULTED, STONE DINING ROOMS would once have been
workshops or sheepfolds, and are often the oldest parts of the houses.
Lined with stone, and often only lit by a single door, the atmosphere
hints at a secret cave dwelling.

THIS SINGLE-STORIED ADDITION has lofty ceilings and expansive living space that incorporates an open-plan kitchen and dining area. Decoration is limited to the natural tones of stone, wood and pale leather. A pair of symmetrical arches leads at one end to the west-facing, conservatory-style breakfast room and, at the other end, to the main drawing room, which is furnished simply with antiques.

AN EIGHTEENTH-CENTURY STONE FIRE SURROUND was bought in
St Rémy. Although most houses are centrally heated, fires are often lit
throughout the sometimes bitterly cold winters. Hanging on the wall
above is a plaster, bas-relief frieze, probably used as a model for
stonecarvers. Unglazed, early twentieth-century Pueblo Indian pots
made of clay and colored with natural pigments adorn a pair of
simple shelves.

WORKS OF ART inject the only colour into these milk-white interiors. *Series Squares* by Ida Kohlmayer dominates the back wall of the drawing room. The rug is a rare 1920s American Navajo Indian piece, and of superb quality.

THE LOW CEILINGS indicate this is the oldest part of the house, the central drawing room features several sets of glass doors leading to the terrace. Contemporary chairs and a sofa facing the seventeenth-century fireplace are covered in white cotton. The long-legged dalmatian is painted papier mâché.

A RUSTIC OLD PROVENÇAL DOOR. next to a
painted screen, leads to the cellar. The walls
have been coloured with yellow ochre, which
has been rubbed on to the plaster to create an
aged finish.

THIS SALON and adjoining kitchen take up the whole of the street-level ground floor. Lit by two pairs of French doors leading to a tiny wrought-iron balconies. Reclaimed nineteenth-century floor tiles have been laid throughout the rooms, providing a richly coloured, cohesive backdrop to a fine collection of regional French furniture and textiles.

RUSTIC BEAMED CEILINGS in the salon are painted the same pale yellow as the walls. A beautifully executed watercolour painting of the property hangs opposite a silk-upholstered sofa piled with fine tapestry cushions.

WITH VIEWS OVER A VALLEY to the south, the ladies' writing room (which is paneled and painted in a soft aqua) is feminine, decorated with fine eighteenth-century furniture and a floral needlepoint carpet. A fine 18C bust and a pair of crystal claret jugs grace a Provencal chest in the mirrored dining alcove.

A FINE EIGHTEENTH-CENTURY STONE FIREPLACE, featuring a central carved shell motif, the symbol of Arles, dominates this first-floor salon. The room forms the third side of the house around a deep courtyard below, and is furnished with a pair of gilt French sofas and an intricately carved and painted bookcase.

ALTHOUGH THE WALLS and massive arches were intact, the floor was just earth, but sensitive restoration has produced a living room of impressive proportion. The room unfolds into several large living rooms by the judicious placing of furniture and rugs in differing groups. A simple galley kitchen is tucked into one corner.

THE ORIGINAL BARN DOORS have been replaced with glass and small windows inserted into the thick stone walls in the dining area, but little light penetrates into the voluminous, cool space. A massive stone fireplace, its scale in keeping with the size of the room, was added during renovation work, along with new, almost white, stone floors. The furnishings are largely French, chosen for shape and large scale, as a room of this size would simply dwarf contemporary pieces.

A STAIRCASE AND MEZZANINE have been added to this salon, providing easy access to the roof terrace. A former workshop is now the winter sitting room. Stripped of crumbling plaster, the walls are left in their original state, although the low arch at the end of the room indicates that at one time this was a much larger space. *Prototype* zebra chairs and a checkered rug from Paris add a whimsical note.

SEVERAL SETS OF FRENCH DOORS, hung with a double-layer of fine Belgian linen, lead from this salon to the broad front terrace. The console table and pair of French fauteuils with needlework upholstery are eighteenth-century. Used for reading and occasional dining, the contemporary Italian hexagonal table was made from old ebony and walnut parquet flooring, bound together with a cast-iron trim.

OLD OAK PLANKS, sanded but not sealed, cover the first floor. A magnificent open-plan room at the top of the staircase is lined with oak cupboards containing a sophisticated home cinema, viewed from a *radassière*, a Turkish daybed draped with an Eastern European velvet patchwork quilt and Venetian velvet cushions.

AS THIS HOUSE is essentially only one room wide, the rooms flow one after the other, each with doors into the garden. Several plate glass windows were replaced to match the original smaller-paned variety. Fortunately, the floor tiles – in various soft ochre shades – were extant. The decoration relies on richly colored textiles, many collected in Laos and other parts of the East.

A WALL OF FRENCH DOORS allows this double
drawing room to extend on to the main terrace
in summer. Books spill out of the library,
bouquets of flowers abound, and plenty of
generous sofas provide seating for large numbers
of people. The colourful picture above the
patterned sofa is by Sylvia Brauerman, bought
from the artist in Vence.

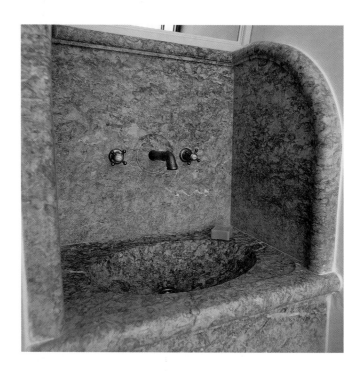

THE CLOAKROOM BASIN, a seventeenth-century design, was made from a local orange marble, and the new taps are copies of those commonly found in Aix-en-Provence. Sarragon marble from the Pyrenees has been used extensively in this master bath and shower room.

TWO MODERN BATHROOMS: A nautical-themed bathroom, where even the floors are a faithful replica of teak ships decking, and another featuring seamless limestone blocks used in a variety of ways. The basin is cut from a single piece of stone and the large shower is hidden behind free-standing wall, also clad in limestone.

A SIMPLE STONE STAIRCASE, worn by centuries of use, leads upwards from the entrance hall. Unadorned walls, and a simple rope handrail, give it a monastic feel.

THE MAIN ENTRANCE leads in all directions with rooms forming an enclosed courtyard linking a separate building to the house. An office and library are set into one corner, straight ahead is an olive planted patio and to the left – down several steps – is the entrance hall. Exterior walls have been cut away at various points along the north side, creating a more formal entry point that was previously confined to the front terrace.

OLD & NEW STAIRCASES: An original staircase and railings (left), alongside a magnificent, new, *Le Baux* stone double- staircase, rising through two floors. The masterly ironwork is an adaptation of an 18C design, similar to overleaf.

LIT ONLY BY A FANLIGHT above the front door, the wide entrance hall is surprisingly light. A nineteenth-century bust greets visitors, and the Papal symbol of Avignon is one of a collection that decorate the hall. The ram's head is North African, but is a common Provençal motif often adorning clay pots.

SHALLOW-TREAD LIMESTONE STAIRS, worn by centuries of use, lead from the tiled entrance hall to the the first floor – a small stained-glass window illuminates the half-landing.

RECLAIMED SEVENTEENTH-CENTURY OAK DOORS lead into the capacious, flagstoned entrance hall. Fine eighteenth-century Burgundy flagstone floors provide the perfect foundation for a collection of superb, mostly antique furniture, including this pair of Louis XVII chairs from a nearby chateau.

BEAUTIFULLY MADE IRONWORK SCREENS and window latches are typical of old Provençal houses. The master bedroom was formerly where the water tanks were housed, but a major redesign of the first-floor rooms created several bedroom and bathroom suites from a warren of smaller rooms. The iron bed was bought in Paris.

BEDROOMS: This guest room features a tiny window and an eighteenth-century fireplace, a simple painted bed and cotton quilt. Antique Chinese priests' chairs, Japanese Imari and a seventeenth-century K'angshi vase, as well as a signed Ming bronze gong, all decorate the master bedroom, above.

BRACQUÉNIE FABRIC is used on the walls and for curtains in this guest bedroom, in classic French style. One of a collection of oriental carpets adorns the tiled floor and an important gilt mirror hangs between a pair of tall, narrow windows. All the furniture is Provençal.

THIS BEAMED-CEILINGED WORKROOM, and guest bedroom, decorated in pale colours, is simply furnished with a painted metal bed and side-table. The elegant, although unadorned, canopy curving over the bed gives a scuptural aspect to the pretty wrought-iron work.

PALE BLUE DOMINATES THIS MASTER BEDROOM. The walls are washed in the lightest tone, antique *toile* and checked linen is used for cushions, and a superb painted dresser with curved drawers makes an ideal dressing table. Original distressed paintwork like this is highly sought after.

TWO GUEST ROOMS, decorated in shades of white, cream and grey-blue, simply furnished with pieces chosen for their good shape and colour, and especially for original paint, no matter whether flaking or worn. Old painted shutters are used as a headboard, their faded grey paintwork toning perfectly with the adjacent portrait.

142

ALL THE BEDROOMS and bathrooms have a country-house feel, where comfort is paramount. Old doors make an effective headboard, and the rough-stone wall, beams and ceiling (opposite) have been painted in a pure, bright white, which creates a romantic feel when teamed with shades of blue.

THE RED AND WHITE FABRIC on the walls is an overscaled embroidery design, the quilt is an English antique, and the bed is nineteenth-century French ironwork. A writing desk is set before a guest-room window overlooking the central courtyard.

STEEPLY PITCHED, white-painted beamed ceilings in the
bedrooms are a counterfoil to the riot of richly colored and
patterned fabrics in reds and yellows.

RUNNING FROM THE FRONT to the back of the house, this kitchen living
space includes an eight-seat fruitwood dining table and painted rush-
seated chairs. All the cupboards – including the enormous one for china
– are painted in a distressed, soft olive green.

PROVENÇAL KITCHENS were never
fitted, but rather furnished with
dressers, shelves and hardy wooden
cupboards that could withstand
constant use. Mesh panels and vivid
paintwork distinguish a cupboard
intended for a dairy. The painted
panel of a woman in traditional
costume has been stuck on to the
door leading to the dining room.

A PAIR OF heavy, VERY OLD STONE SINKS are set into the work counters at either end of the kitchen and, so large is the space that, a sixteen-seat table sits easily between. Walls of antique cupboards are filled with china, while fabric-lined cupboards hold glassware and hide fridges.

THIS KITCHEN is filled with over-scaled pieces collected from all over the world. The tabletop is part of an old painted ceiling, a cherry and elmwood draper's table from Lyon fills one wall, and wooden Spanish window trellis adds depth to the blank walls behind the kitchen counter. The collection of enormous amber and green glass vinegar bottles are from Trinquetaille, across the Rhône. Old silver and antique china form an effective still life on the draper's table.

159

WITH A LOW CEILING and original, gigantic stone fireplace, this was the heart of the old house. French oak and volcanic slate were used to make the table, while the chairs are 1920s *American Arts and Crafts*. Terriers sleep in specially made houses under the handmade tiled worktop.

ROUGH STONE WALLS have been left unplastered in the kitchen. The soft
terracotta wash on the walls extends to the inner hall and staircase
leading to bedrooms on the first floor, while the cupboards are painted
a similar grey-green to the shutters hung at all the windows across the
front of the house.

A NEW KITCHEN in an older style was created in the centre of this
house, lit by removing a section of the outer wall and replacing it
with glass. Every effort has been made to use traditional local
materials – the custom-made stone sink, the wall tiles, cupboards
and carved chandelier all came from nearby villages.

ENTERED FROM A SHELTERED, covered terrace, the kitchen has plenty of simple open shelving, used for storage. Massive square beams run lengthwise through the kitchen and adjoining dining room. The wood and zinc bar counter is said to have been rescued from a fire in Lacoste's Café de France fifty years ago.

LANDSCAPE ENTERPRISE LTD
Rue Basse
Lacoste 84480
Tel 00 33 490 75 86 34
Fax 00 33 490 75 88 09
e-mail alex@admgarden.com
Alex Dingwall-Main, Garden
architect and designer. Author of
the Lubéron Garden (2002), and
The Angel Tree(2003) Ebury
Press.

FRENCH COUNTRY LIVING
21, Rue De L'Eglise
Mougins 06250
Tel 00 33 493 75 53 03
Douglas and Jean Hill, antiques
dealers specialising in French and
Italian furniture often with
original paintwork – decorative
items, mirrors and old linens.

DECORACION et JARDINS
3, Place des Trois Ormeaux
Aix-en-Provence 13100
Tel 00 33 442 35232
Jean-Louis Raynaud and Kenyon
Kramer. International interior and
garden designers.

DAVID PRICE
Mas des Chataigniers
Chemin du Grava
Le Paradou 13520 – near St.
Rémy-de-Provence

Tel 00 33 490 54 30 04
e-mail aprice@club-internet.fr
David Price - Architectural
building and renovation business
for international clients
throughout Provence. Expert on
sourcing local materials and
reclaimed items, interior
planning/design and high quality
finishes.

DOMAINE DU GRAND CROS
Rte de Carnoules 83890
Besse-sur-Issole
Var
Tel 00 33 498 01 80 08
e-mail jhf@grandcros.fr
Hon Hugh J. Jane and Julian
Faulkner – Winemakers.

**BRUNO & ALEXANDRE
LAFOURCADE**
Bureau D'Etudes
10, Boulevard Victor Hugo
Saint-Rémy-de-Provence 13210
Tel 00 33 490 92 10 14
Fax 00 33 490 92 49 72
Bruno Lafourcade – Architecture
and design studio specialising in
all areas of traditional Provençal
country house renovation, re-
design and building. Dominic
Lafourcade, garden designer and
artist.

Barbara Ther
Les Muriers
Uzes
Robert Hering and Jim Stringer
Mas du Manescau
Saint-Rémy-du-Provence

LES MAS DES GRES
Hotel de charme
Route d'Apt RN 100
F-84800 Lagnes near l'Isle-sur-la-
Sorgue
Tel 00 33 490 20 21 45
Fax 00 33 490 20 21 45
e-mail info@masdesgres.com
Nina & Thierry Crovara, the best
kitchen in Vaucluse.

**TIM REES AND BRITA VON
SCHOENAICH**
149 Liverpool Road
London N1 0RF
Tel 00 44 207 837 3800
Major garden design, construction
and planting undertaken
throughout Provence.

ROBERT DALLAS
Cabinet d'architecture
Domaine de Notre Dame
06570 Saint-Paul-de-Vence
Tel 00 33 494 32 55 55
e-mail rd@dallas.com